So how do you tell insects and arachnids apart?

The easiest way is to count the number of legs, body bits or eyes they have:

I have six legs!

Ha! I've got eight!

So what? I can fly!

Yeah . . . but can you hang from a silk thread coming out of your bum — and then eat your way back up it again at high speed?

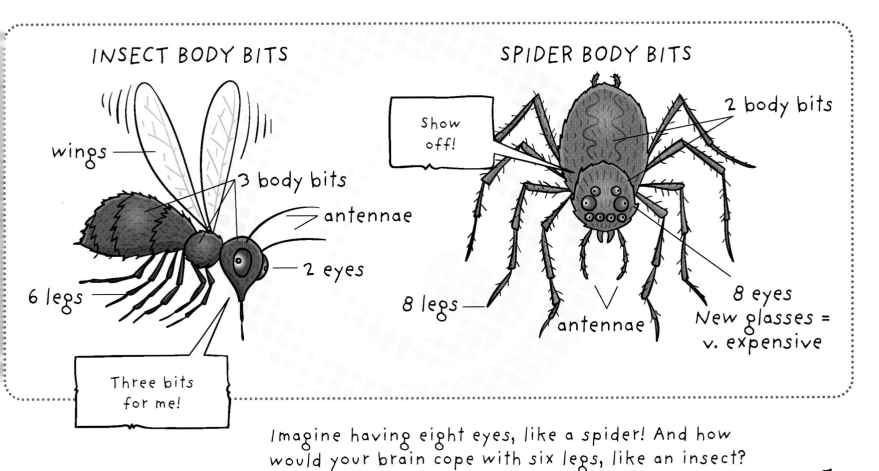

INSECT BODY BITS

wings

3 body bits

antennae

2 eyes

6 legs

Three bits for me!

SPIDER BODY BITS

Show off!

2 body bits

8 legs

antennae

8 eyes
New glasses = v. expensive

Imagine having eight eyes, like a spider! And how would your brain cope with six legs, like an insect?

# BUG NOISE

Bugs can make all kinds of really odd noises — including some quite confusing ones.

## RATTLING CICADA

Sounds like: a rattlesnake behind you

Is: a male cicada looking for a girlfriend

Cicadas can shake their rattles 350 times a second. The noise can be louder than city-centre traffic.

AAAAH! RATTLESNAKE!

Rattle Rattle Rattle

It always gets them rattled!

F Y

I S

By Paul Mason and Tony De Saulles

WAYLAND

First published in Great Britain in 2023
by Wayland
Text and Design Copyright © Hodder and Stoughton, 2023
Illustrations Copyright © Tony De Saulles, 2023

Editor: Grace Glendinning
Designer: Peter Scoulding

HBK ISBN: 978 1 5263 2229 6
PBK ISBN: 978 1 5263 2230 2
EBK ISBN: 978 1 5263 2582 2

Printed and bound in China

Wayland, an imprint of
Hachette Children's Group
Part of Hodder and Stoughton
Carmelite House
50 Victoria Embankment
London EC4Y 0DZ

An Hachette UK Company
www.hachette.co.uk
www.hachettechildrens.co.uk

# CONTENTS

# IT'S A BUGGY WORLD

What is a bug? In this book, bugs are insects and arachnids. There are ZILLIONS* of them out there. Bugs make up over half the species on our planet.

Bugs are at or near the bottom of almost every food chain. They also help plants reproduce. Without bugs, life on Earth would not exist.

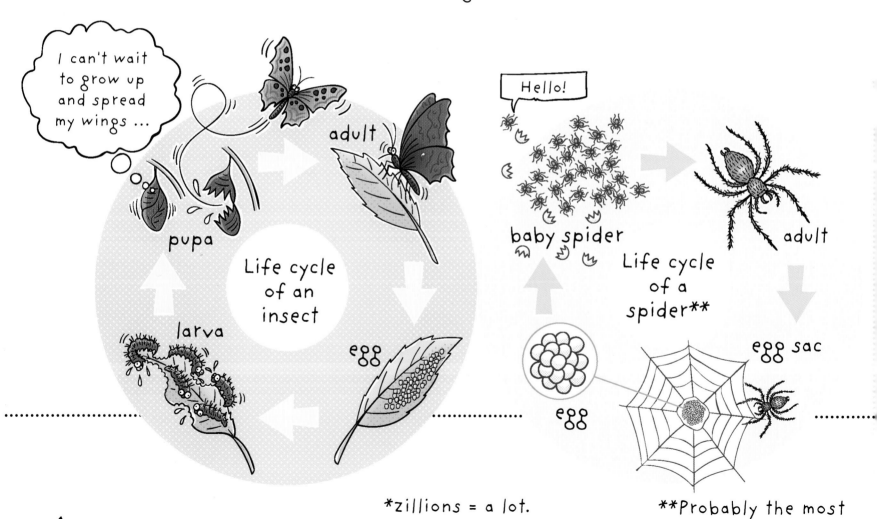

I can't wait to grow up and spread my wings ...

adult

pupa

Life cycle of an insect

larva

egg

Hello!

baby spider

adult

Life cycle of a spider**

egg sac

egg

*zillions = a lot. REALLY a lot.

**Probably the most famous arachnid.

# CLICK-BEETLE RESCUE

For a beetle, ending up on your back is a disaster. Flipping back is either tricky or impossible. That leaves lots of time for something to come and eat you.

Unless you are a click beetle ...

BRRRING,
BRRRING,
BRRRING...

Is that your mum calling AGAIN?

No, it's my dad!

Oh no ...

Bends one way ... CLICK!

LIFT OFF!

... and snaps back.

That's better.

# THE RINGTONE CRICKET

Sounds like: old-fashioned ringtone

Is: a male snowy tree cricket making signal noises

Whirring wings make noise

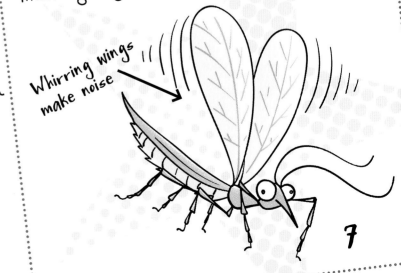

7

# NEEDLE-NOSED BUGS

Some bugs have evolved to have super-long snouts, which they use in all kinds of unexpected ways.

LANTERNFLY

This lanternfly looks a bit snooty, with its upturned nose.

In fact, the lanternfly uses its nose to dig through tree bark, then suck out sugary juice from inside.

I'm not a snob! I'm just thirsty.

Ouch! Stick your nose somewhere else!

Reusable drinking straw attached

SLURP!

# MOSQUITO

Meet the most annoying needle-nosed bug of all — the female mosquito.

**SUCK! SUCK!**

Female mosquito

Needle nose

Blood sucked into abdomen

Male mosquitoes do not drink blood. Instead, they only suck up plant nectar.

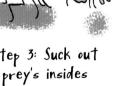

Stand back. This is men's work!

NOW who's annoying?!

# ASSASSIN BUG

You can probably guess from their name that assassin bugs do not play well with others ...

oof.

## THE ASSASSIN BUG MAKES LUNCH

GAH!

Step 1: Spear prey

Erk!

Step 2: Inject digestive juice into prey

Mmm!

Step 3: Suck out prey's insides

# BUGS THAT PULL FACES

If you're a bug, there's always someone trying to eat you. These bugs have found an excellent way of facing this problem.

## SNAKE-MIMIC CATERPILLAR

This tricky caterpillar loves doing impressions — but it can only do one: a snake. Not everyone likes the impression, either.

A yummy snack ...

I mean SNAKE!

I'm actually a peace-loving plant eater ...

We are the Happy Face Family — SMILE AND BE PROUD!

UGGGHH, WHATEVER!

Not all the markings look like smiles. Some even appear to frown.

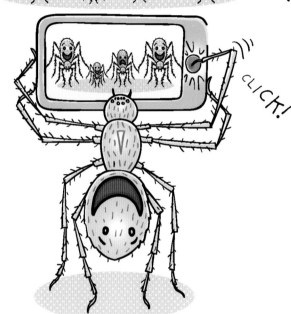

CLICK!

# HAWAIIAN HAPPY FACE SPIDER

No one is 100% sure why the happy-face spider wears a happy face on its back. Is it because it's lucky enough to live in Hawaii?

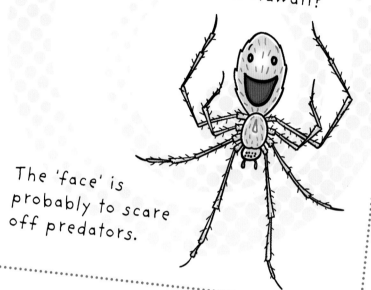

The 'face' is probably to scare off predators.

# PUSS-MOTH CATERPILLAR

OF COURSE a caterpillar that looks as though it's wearing lipstick is funny.

I disagree.

When threatened, these caterpillars raise their heads and wave their pink-tipped tails around.

If that doesn't work, they have a second defence ...

LIPSTICK POWER!

Formic acid spray

11

# BUG EYES

Some bugs are harder to sneak up on than others. Flies, for example, can see in almost a complete circle. That's what makes them so hard to swat!

## JUMPING SPIDER

Jumping spiders have some of the best vision in the bug world.

The little eyes on the sides of their heads spot prey. Then the spider turns so the big eyes in the middle can lock on to its victim.

turns to line eyes up

# MONKEY GRASSHOPPER

The monkey grasshopper's eyes are for spotting predators — which is why they are huge and on the side of its head.

Birds, spiders, wasps and small animals love to eat grasshoppers.

No wonder it looks so worried.

Don't give me that! I INVENTED side-eye.

# STALK-EYED FLY

Stalk-eyed flies form their eye stalks just after they emerge from the pupa.

While their skin and flesh are still soft, they pump air into the stalks, which grow out like long party balloons.

Don't overfill them, son — THEY'LL POP!

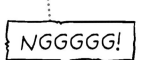

NGGGGG!

13

# BUGS IN DISGUISE, PART 1

For a hungry predator bug, one good way to get a meal is to disguise yourself as something innocent.

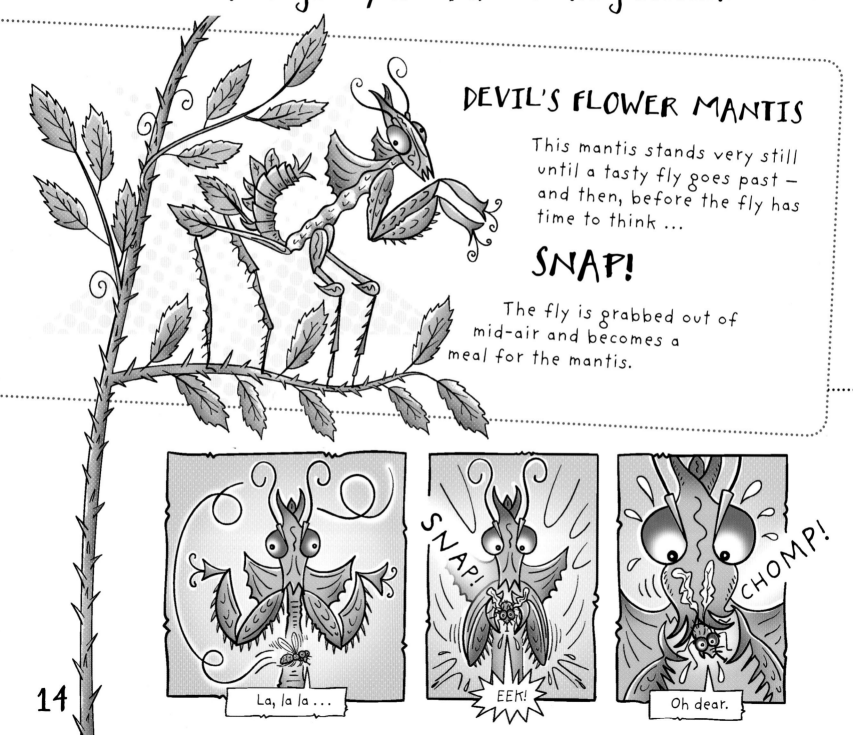

## DEVIL'S FLOWER MANTIS

This mantis stands very still until a tasty fly goes past — and then, before the fly has time to think ...

## SNAP!

The fly is grabbed out of mid-air and becomes a meal for the mantis.

La, la la ...

SNAP!

EEK!

CHOMP!

Oh dear.

## ACANTHASPIS PETAX

Acanthaspis petax disguises itself under a ball of the dead bodies of its prey (ants).

Scientists used to think this was a hunting technique — but it's actually to AVOID being hunted itself, by jumping spiders.

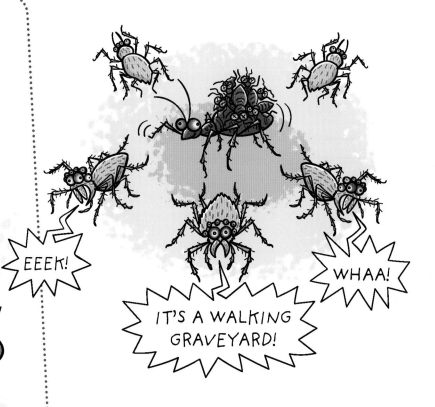

EEEK!

IT'S A WALKING GRAVEYARD!

WHAA!

YAARGH! I'm naked without my mask!

## MASKED HUNTER BUG

The masked hunter isn't naturally well-camouflaged — at least, not until it covers itself with dust, dirt and sand to blend in with its background.

What do you mean, "bath night"?

15

# BUGS IN DISGUISE, PART 2

## Some bug disguises take it to the next level.

### BIRD-DUNG CRAB SPIDER

It might not seem a good idea to LOOK AND SMELL like bird poo, but if you're a tiny spider it:

a)    puts off predators (e.g. birds), and ALSO

b)    attracts the moths you like to eat.

Spider. Not poo.

Smells nice!

These two are BOTH birdbrains ...

Yuk!

That is definitely NOT dinner.

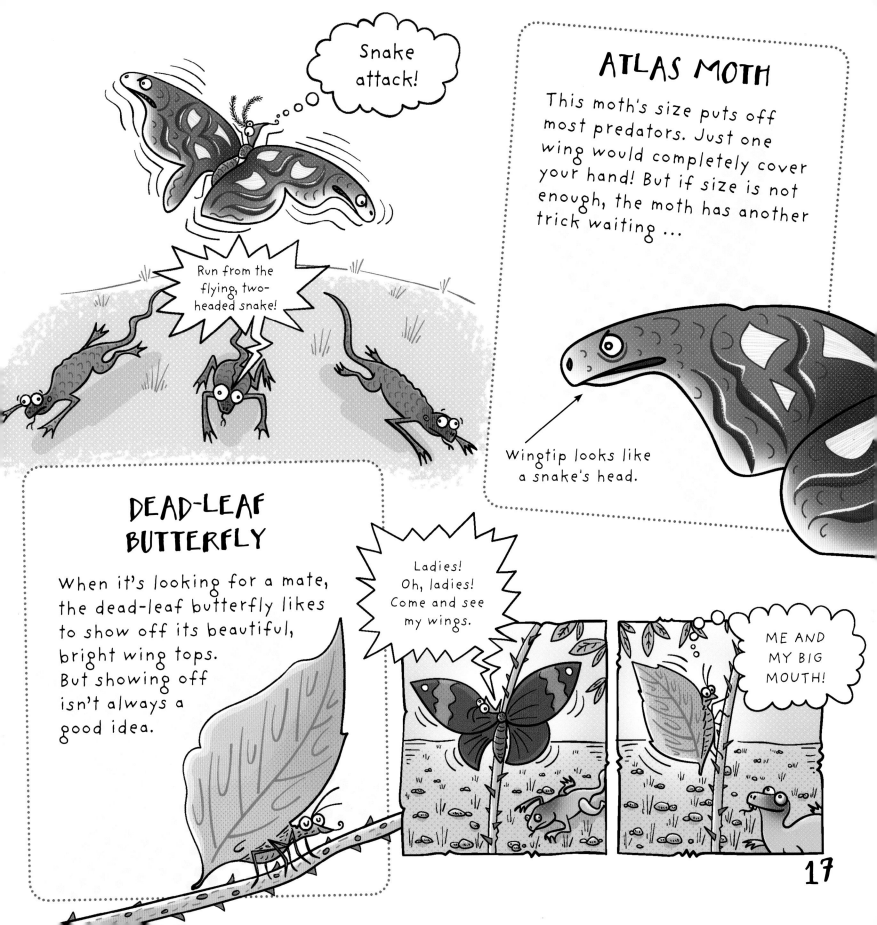

Snake attack!

## ATLAS MOTH

This moth's size puts off most predators. Just one wing would completely cover your hand! But if size is not enough, the moth has another trick waiting ...

Wingtip looks like a snake's head.

Run from the flying, two-headed snake!

## DEAD-LEAF BUTTERFLY

When it's looking for a mate, the dead-leaf butterfly likes to show off its beautiful, bright wing tops. But showing off isn't always a good idea.

Ladies! Oh, ladies! Come and see my wings.

ME AND MY BIG MOUTH!

17

# THE BIGGEST BUGS

Certain beetles are among the biggest bugs of all. You had better hope one of these doesn't crawl into your tent on a camping holiday ...

## GOLIATH BEETLE

These beetles are fierce: their Y-shaped horns are used for fighting other goliaths. They grow biggest in captivity, after being fed dog or cat food.

I'm also winner of the World's Strongest Beetle competition.*

Hang on ... That's MY dinner.

It's MY dinner now, friend.

*Not a real competition.

# HERCULES BEETLE

Male hercules beetles are the longest beetles in the world.

Males are also the judo stars of the beetle world. They fight by trying to pick up their opponents and throwing them through the air.

> Hai-YAH!

> Wish I'd known he was a black belt ...

> Actually, it was ME that won World's Strongest Beetle.**

**Still not a real competition.

# RHINOCEROS COCKROACH

If you don't like cockroaches, look away now.

This one is so big it would cover the palm of your hand. Even so, they are popular pets, as they are clean and do not bite.

> He hisses through his bottom when he's nervous!

> ME TOO!

Bring a Pet to School Day

HISS!

PFFF!

# STINKING BUGS

These bugs should be top of your list of "Bugs to Avoid if You Don't Like to be Sprayed with Stinky or Stinging Stuff".

## MAN-FACED STINK BUG

We all know stink bugs stink. But the most fun thing about the man-faced stink bug is that it's the *Elvis impersonator* of the bug world.

Whenever they find a new food source, stink bugs also release a chemical signal to tell their friends.

Wingtips like a 1950s haircut

Markings on back look like a face.

STINK!

It's not every day Elvis invites you to dinner ...

Munch! Munch!

Thanks for the tip on lunch, Elvis!

20

## VIOLIN BEETLE

These beetles live underneath tree bark and are almost flat.

They like a quiet life — so they squirt stinging fluid into the eyes of anyone who bothers them.

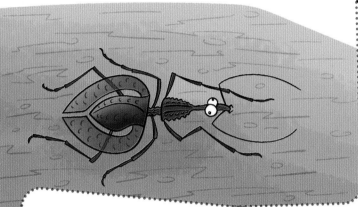

## AUSTRALIAN WALKING STICK

Female Australian walking sticks are too heavy to escape danger by flying — but they have other ways of putting off attackers ...

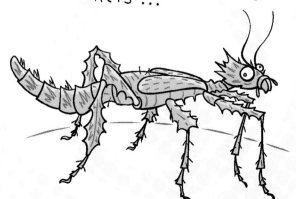

21

# CONFUSING CATERPILLARS

There are some loony-looking larvae around. These caterpillars are either dangerous, tricky ... or both.

## FLANNEL-MOTH CATERPILLAR

This caterpillar is sometimes called the Puss caterpillar.

**Looks:** cosy, furry and strokeable.

**Actually:** the 'hairs' are oozing with venom. Stroking it (or if you are a bird, trying to eat it) is a <u>Bad Idea</u>.

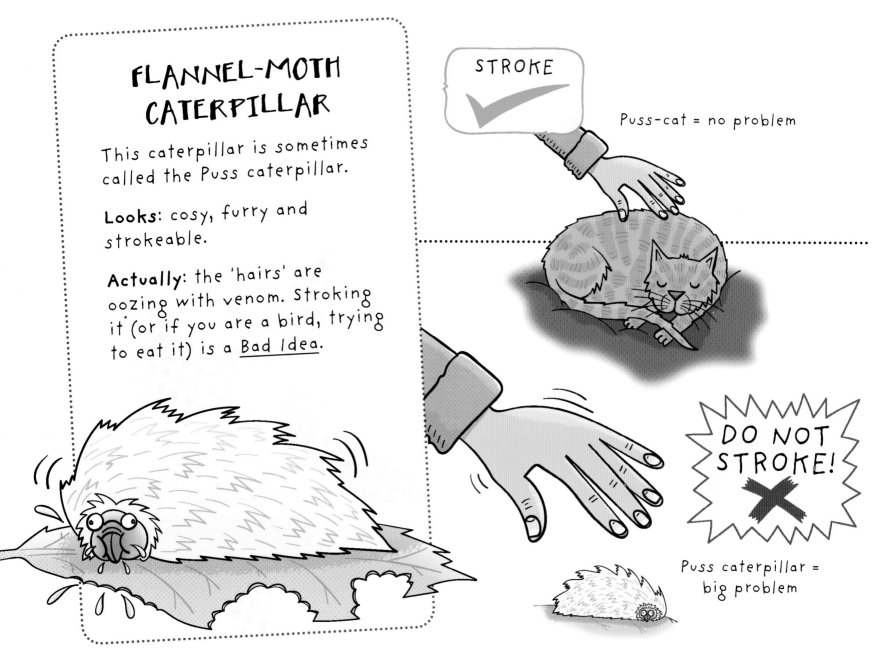

STROKE ✓

Puss-cat = no problem

DO NOT STROKE! ✗

Puss caterpillar = big problem

The green colour isn't icing!

The dots on its face aren't eyes!

The face isn't a face!

IT'S ALL LIES!

## SADDLEBACK CATERPILLAR

**Looks:** bright green and a bit like a tasty sweet.

**Actually:** covered with poisonous spines and NOT good to eat.

WHAT ARE YOU STARING AT?

## IO MOTH CATERPILLAR

This little bug keeps it weird its whole life:

- its 8-day-old eggs look like human eyeballs lying around

- its caterpillar turns bright green in later stages

- the actual moth's wings STARE at YOU with fake eyes.

# DANCING BUGS

Doing a little dance is a GREAT way to show how pleased you are to see someone. Just ask these bugs ...

## PEACOCK SPIDER DISCO

When a male peacock spider catches the eye of a female, IT'S DISCO TIME:

1) He waves his black-and-white stripy legs over his head.

2) He flicks up a colourful, shimmery disc and flaps it about in the air.

Each species of peacock spider has its own unique dance.

Honestly ... the sparklemuffin* peacock spider wins EVERY year.

SPIDERS GOT SKILLS

MATE    KILL

TA-DAAA!

*This species really exists, and does the most remarkable dance.

24

# WALTZING SCORPIONS

Some scorpion species do a mating dance, holding claws and moving around as if they are waltzing.

And ONE-two-three, ONE-two-three, ONE-two-three!

I thought I was leading?

# TAP-DANCING LACEWINGS

Lacewing flies always go dancing on a first date. They meet ... then start to tap out a rhythm with their abdomens.

A second date only happens if their tapping rhythms match.

25

# BUG LOVE

Doing a special dance (as on page 24) is not the ONLY way for a bug to find a girlfriend or boyfriend ...

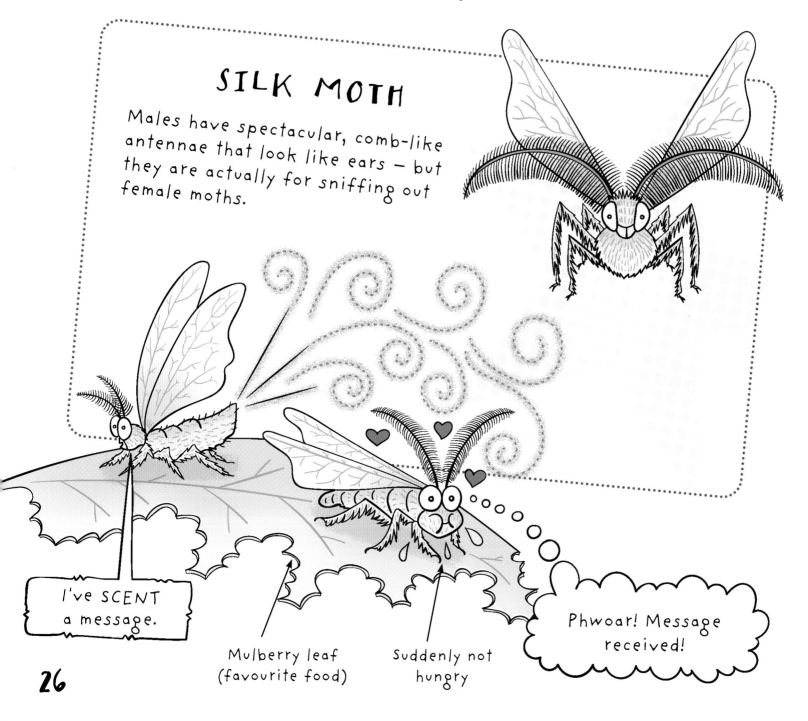

## SILK MOTH

Males have spectacular, comb-like antennae that look like ears — but they are actually for sniffing out female moths.

I've SCENT a message.

Mulberry leaf (favourite food)

Suddenly not hungry

Phwoar! Message received!

# SCORPION FLY

Males use their tails to show off to females. If she is not impressed, though, she might eat him! To avoid this, he brings her presents — such as a dead insect to eat, or a big glob of saliva.

I hope you like them.

Fruit fly and drool — my favourites!

# ORCHID BEE

Male orchid bees spend weeks gathering scents from different plants, to make what they hope is the perfect perfume.

They store it in their back legs — then fly about hoping to meet a female who also loves the scent.

SNIFF... UGH!

SNIFF... YUK!

SNIFF... I LOVE IT!

# MORE FUNNY BUGS

These funny bugs are either scary, mysterious ...
or just plain goofy.

## WRAP-AROUND SPIDER

This little spider's belly curves inwards, which means it can wrap itself tightly around branches. It blends in so well that predatory birds cannot see it.

Listen to ME
My name is Spi-DEE.
What's going DOWN
Is I'm rapping all a-ROUN!

Not that kind of rap, you wally!

## VELVET ANTS

The first funny thing about these insects is their name: they are not ants, but wasps. They come in all shapes and colours, but the only ones that sting are the females ... and they can't fly!

GRRR — MEN! ALWAYS TEASING US THAT WE CAN'T FLY.

MAKES ME WANT TO STING THEM!

# ORB-WEAVER SPIDERS

No one is sure why these freaky fellows look the way they do — but their special features would definitely make them hard to eat.

Long-horned orb-weaver

Spiny-backed orb-weaver

# JEWEL CATERPILLAR

These caterpillars are almost see-through — apart from little coloured, gooey knobs all along their backs, which easily break off, giving attackers a face full of goo.

# APHID-MILKING ANTS

Ants trap aphids by tranquillising them, then cutting off their wings.

Then the ants stroke the aphids to make them release sweet honeydew — which the ants slurp up.

# BUGS QUIZ

**1  Why don't spiders wear glasses?**

  a) They don't have noses on which to balance glasses.

  b) Spiders have eight eyes so it would be too expensive.

  c) Spiders hate taking eye tests and always refuse to go.

**2  What's a good way for a vulnerable bug to stop itself being eaten?**

  a) Adopt a disguise (for example, look like a snake or a poo).

  b) Cover itself in something horrid (such as sticky gunk or poison).

  c) Squirt acid at anyone who threatens it.

  d) All of those.

**3  Are sparklemuffin spiders ...**

  a) Spiders with bright, sparkly eyes and a friendly personality

  b) Spiders that look like a colourful cake

  c) The spider world's best dancers?

**4  Which bugs should dogs avoid?**

  a) Flannel-moth caterpillars, because sniffing them could poison their nose.

  b) Violin beetles, because if they get too close they will squirt acid at them.

  c) Goliath beetles, because they are partial to dog food and might steal their dinner.

  d) All of those!

**5  One last question: which is your favourite bug in this book?**

There is no right or wrong answer to this question — but all the other answers are below, upside-down.

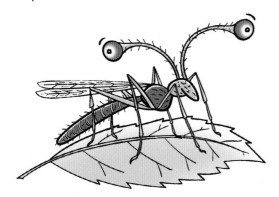

**Answers**

1: a) and b) (spiders don't have noses, and they do have eight eyes).

2: d) (you can find bugs in this book that defend themselves in all these ways).

3: c) (if there was a spider Strictly Come Dancing, the sparklemuffin would probably win every time).

4: d) (use the index to see where you can find out about these bugs, if you haven't already).

30

# GLOSSARY

**acid** stinging and unpleasant substance. Some acids are able to melt living things, or even metals

**assassin** ruthless killer

**caterpillar** larva of a butterfly or moth

**Elvis** Elvis Presley, the world's biggest music star in the 1950s and 1960s

**food chain** line of plants and animals where each living thing depends on the one before it for food

**iridescent** with bright, shining colours that seem to change depending on the angle you look at them

**larva** third stage in the life of many insects, after egg and pupa, but before adult

**mate** begin the process of creating young

**predator** animal that hunts other animals for food

**pupa** second stage in the life of many insects, after egg and before larva and adult

**species** group of living things that look alike and are able to have young together

**spine** spike; hard object with a wider base and a pointed tip

**tranquillise** make calm or quieten

**venom** poison that is injected after a bite or sting

## FURTHER READING

For more fun nature reading, why not try these other awesome books?

The **Body Bits** series, by Paul Mason and Dave Smith, Wayland 2020

- *Hair-raising Human Body Facts*
  9781526312891 Paperback

- *Astounding Animal Body Facts*
  9781526313447 Paperback

- *Eye-popping Plant Part Facts*
  9781526314659 Paperback

- *Dead-awesome Dinosaur Body Facts*
  9781526315175 Paperback

The **Animals Do** series, by Paul Mason, Tony De Saulles and Gemma Hastilow, Wayland 2018–2022

- *The Poo that Animals Do*
  9781526303950 Paperback

- *The Wee that Animals Pee*
  9781526309730 Paperback

- *The Farts that Animals Parp*
  9781526312235 Paperback

- *The Snot that Animals Have Got*
  9781526317100 Paperback

31

# INDEX